Howard Patterson

**Yacht Etiquette**

Courtesies, Discipline, Ceremonies, and Routine for Any and...

Howard Patterson

**Yacht Etiquette**
*Courtesies, Discipline, Ceremonies, and Routine for Any and...*

ISBN/EAN: 9783744791649

Printed in Europe, USA, Canada, Australia, Japan

Cover: Foto ©Andreas Hilbeck / pixelio.de

More available books at **www.hansebooks.com**

# YACHT ETIQUETTE.

Courtesies, Discipline, Ceremonies
and Routine for Any and
All Circumstances.

Duties of Officers, etc.

BY

CAPTAIN HOWARD PATTERSON,

*Principal of the New York Nautical College.
Formerly Commander of the New York School Ship
"St. Mary's", Master of Various Sail and Steam Yachts,
and Admiral of the Haytien Navy.*

AUTHOR OF

*The Navigator's Pocket-Book; Yachting Under American
Statute; The Illustrated Nautical Dictionary; Hand
Book for Masters and Mates, etc.*

PUBLISHED BY

The New York Nautical College,
130 & 132 Water Street,    New York City.

PRESS OF
E. S. MAYO
9 WARREN ST.
NEW YORK

*To My Friend*
HOWARD GOULD

*Sincerely Yours,
Howard Patterson*

# PREFACE.

It is to be understood that the owner of the yacht is styled as "Captain" throughout this treatise, and it is eminently proper that this should be, as the Government prescribes that the owner of a yacht is entitled to take out her custom house and other papers as the lawful and legalized "Master" of his vessel.

It being impracticable to follow out naval rules strictly in the matter of salutes, courtesies, ceremonies, etc., a modification of the same has been arranged which will cover the requirements of yachting and contribute dignity to such observances as are called for in the foregoing.

As stated under the head of "Duties and Responsibilities of Officers", the rules and regulations laid down specially refer to the larger class of steam yachts, but it is explained that these laws may be modified to apply to smaller classes of pleasure vessels.

# CONTENTS.

| | |
|---|---:|
| COLORS IN GENERAL, | 9 |
| SPECIAL LIGHTS, | 23 |
| OFFICIAL CEREMONIES AND COURTESIES, | 25 |
| SALUTES IN GENERAL, | 34 |
| BOAT SERVICE, | 40 |
|     Particulars concerning Boats, | 40 |
|     Boat Ceremony and Discipline, | 43 |
|     Boat Orders, | 44 |
|     Boat Salutes, | 47 |
| SHIP'S BELLS, | 55 |
| THE BOATSWAIN'S CALL, | 57 |
| YACHT ROUTINE, | 60 |

DUTIES AND RESPONSIBILITIES OF
OFFICERS:

| | |
|---|---:|
| Captain, | 69 |
| Sailing-Master, | 74 |
| Chief Engineer, | 77 |
| First Mate, | 83 |
| Second Mate, | 85 |
| Boatswain, | 87 |
| Carpenter, | 89 |
| Quartermasters, | 91 |
| Steward, | 92 |
| Surgeon, | 96 |

# YACHT ETIQUETTE.

## COLORS IN GENERAL.

*Time to Make Colors-- Place to Display Same.* When at anchor or underway, the ensign of a yacht in commission should be hoisted at 8 A. M. and kept flying until sunset. When at anchor it is hoisted on the flag pole at the stern of both steam and sail yachts, and when underway it is hoisted to the after gaff-end on sailing vessels; but is usually retained on the pole in the case of steam yachts, although it may be hoisted to the gaff-end if desired. The burgee should be hoisted to the fore topmast head on schooners, and the private signal at the main topmast.

**Senior Officer Present to Give the Time for Colors and Sunset.**
The time for making colors and sunset should be taken from the senior officer's yacht present, whether he is on board or not, and the only gun fired for colors and sunset should be the one on such senior's yacht.

**At Anchor with Naval Vessel or off a Naval Station.**
When a yacht is in company with a vessel of her own navy, or at anchor off a naval station, the senior officer present should regulate the time for colors and sunset to such vessel or station.

**Visiting Home Waters of Another Yacht Club.**
Yachts visiting the home waters of another club (provided such waters are other than their own) should take their time for colors and sunset from the yacht of the senior officer of such club present.

**Entering Port Before Colors or After Sunset.**
When a yacht enters port in the morning before colors are made, or in the evening

after sunset, her ensign, club burgee and private signal should be displayed and kept flying until the yacht comes to anchor, when they should be hauled down.

Night Pennant. During the night (between sunset and colors) the yacht should fly a night pennant at the main topmast head.

Absence Pennant. During the absence of the captain from the yacht, a blue rectangular flag (called Absence Pennant) should be kept flying at the starboard main spreader. The private signal (or flag officer's pennant) however, is to be kept flying whether the captain is on board or not.

Single Stickers--Where, When and How to Fly Burgee and Private Signal. Single masted vessels should not fly the private signal on the same halliards as the club burgee. If one of the two flags only is to be shown, then it should be the private signal when entering a home port of the club, or when at sea. Entering a foreign port (any port other than her own) the yacht should fly the club burgee.

Meal Pennants. During the meal hours of the captain, when the yacht is at anchor, a white rectangular flag should be flown at the starboard main spreader, and during the meal hours of the crew a red pennant should be flown from the port fore spreader. Of course, on a "single sticker" the white flag and red meal pennant must both be flown from the same mast, but they will be exhibited on their proper sides. After colors a white light should be shown from the starboard main spreader to indicate that the captain is at dinner. Meal flags should not be flown when the yacht is underway.

Colors to be Flown in Gig. The yacht's gig, when brought to the gangway or is away from the yacht, shall display the ensign at the stern. While the captain is in the gig, the private signal should be displayed at the bow. If a club member is in the boat without the captain, a club burgee should be displayed at the bow.

**Flag Officer's Pennant.** Flag officers fly a pennant at the main on yachts and on the forward flag-staff of gigs, to distinguish their rank. These pennants take the place of the yacht's private signal.

**Yacht Short Handed.** If the yacht is short handed, two flags may be bent on to the same set of halliards, so that while one flag is being sent aloft the other may be coming down.

**Burgee and Private Signal May be Broken Out.** The club burgee and private signal may be "made up" and mastheaded previous to colors, and "broken out" when the signal for colors is given.

**Colors to be Well Hoisted.** Daylight should never show between the head of a flag and the truck.

**National Mourning.** On occasions of national mourning the ensign should be half-masted, but the burgee and private signal should be kept mast-headed.

**Death of Captain.** In the event of the death of the captain on shore, both the club burgee and private signal of his yacht should be kept half-masted from colors until sunset on the day of the funeral, but the ensign should be kept fully hoisted during the same time. If, on the other hand, the death should occur on board while the yacht is in port, then the ensign also should be half-masted as soon as the body leaves the vessel for the shore, and the ensign should be kept so flying until sunset of the same day. Should the burial of the captain take place at sea, then the ensign of the vessel and the captain's private signal should be displayed at half-mast at the commencement of the ceremony and kept flying until its conclusion, when the ensign and private signal should be hauled down.

**Death of Flag Officer.** On the occasion of the death of a flag officer while his yacht is in port, his pennant should be hauled down at sunset on the day of his funeral, and should not be again hoisted — the yacht's private signal taking its place. If the funeral takes place at sea, then the pennant should be hauled down with the ensign at the conclusion of the ceremonies.

**Death of Club Member.** When mourning is ordered for the death of a club member, the burgee only is half-masted, and this should be observed, whether underway or at anchor.

**How to Half-Mast Colors.** The ensign, burgee and private signal (also flag-officer's pennant) should always be mast-headed before they are half-masted.

**Saluting with Ensign at Half-Mast.** Whenever it becomes necessary to salute with the flag while the ensign is flying at half-mast, it must be mast-headed before it is dipped.

**Hauling Down Half-Mast Colors.** Before hauling down half-masted colors, always mast-head them first.

**Death of One of the Crew.** In the event of the death of the sailing master, mate, or other officer, or one of the crew at sea, the ensign of the yacht should be half-masted during the funeral ceremony. Should the death of one of the above occur on board while the yacht is in port, then the ensign should be half-masted from the time that the body leaves the yacht until the body is landed or until the return of the boat that conveyed the body to the shore.

**Permission to Half-Mast Colors to be Obtained.** No yacht of a fleet other than that of the senior officer present should ever half-mast her colors until permission to do so has been obtained.

**Hours for Half-Masting Colors.** Funeral honors in the way of half-masting colors should not be paid before sunrise nor after sunset.

**Boat Engaged in Funeral Ceremony.** When a boat is engaged in funeral ceremonies in conveying a body to the shore, the ensign in the stern should be kept half-masted until the body is landed.

**Making Colors.** About five minutes before colors, have the club and private signals, night pennant, and ensign (also absence flag, if owner is not on board) halliards manned, the boat-boom guys tended, and a hand stationed at the ship's bell. As soon as the signal is given for colors, call: "Strike eight bells and hoist away!" At this instant swing out the boat-booms, haul down the night pennant, and send aloft the bunting.

**Making Sunset.** About fifteen minutes before the time given for sunset, have the anchor light, gangway light, and signal light or lights all ready, the boats either hoisted or dropped astern, and the night pennant bent on. About five minutes before sunset, station the men at the boom-guys, club, and private signals and ensign halliards (also absence flag halliards if the captain is not on board), anchor light whip, gangway light, and captain's distinguishing light or lights. If you are the flagship you will also have a gunner stationed at the off-shore gun, and wait, watch in hand (care should be observed to have it on correct local time) for the time given for sunset. But if you are taking time from another vessel, or from the shore, the time need not concern you; simply await the sunset signal, then call: "Haul down!" At this instant let go the forward boat-boom guys and swing the booms in. Observe that the club, private signal, absence flag and ensign, are hauled down (the two former preserving the same height to one another until they reach the deck) and that the night pennant and anchor light go aloft as soon as the order to haul down is given. Arrange the captain's signal lantern or lanterns, and the gangway light, and make the bunting up neatly and stow it away in the flag locker. If the boats are riding astern, give them a short painter to prevent them from being run over by vessels coming in to anchor, or passing under your stern.

Day Signals for Pilots. The following signals, numbered 1 and 2, when displayed together or separately, shall be deemed to be signals for a pilot, in the day time :—1st, To be hoisted at the fore, the Jack or other national color usually worn by merchant ships, having round it a white border one-fifth of the breadth of the flag; or, 2nd, The International Code Pilotage Signal, indicated by P. T.

Night Signals for Pilots. The following signals, numbered 1 and 2, when used or displayed together, or separately, shall be deemed to be signals for a pilot, in the night time :— 1st, The pyrotechnic light, commonly known as a blue light, every fifteen minutes; or, 2nd, a bright white light, flashed or shown at short intervals, just above the bulwarks, for about a minute at a time.

Signal for Towing Boat. The signal for a towing boat is made by setting the ensign in the main rigging a little way above the deck.

Dressing Ship. The prettiest mode of dressing a ship with flags is to make an arch of them from the jib-boom end to the fore-top-masthead, thence across to the maintop-masthead, and down to the main-boom end, allowing two or more flags to hang down under the jib-boom end and the main-boom end respectively, with a lead attached to the end of each line to keep the flags from flying around. Hoisted to the trucks, by the regular signal halliards, should be the ensign, Jack, or the flags of the nation in whose port the ship is lying, or the distinguishing flags of the person whom it is desired to honor. The arch of flags should be hoisted so as to give the former flags room to display themselves. Have blocks at the topmast-heads for the fore and aft strings of arch flags, and hoist the flags to them by means of a whip. The flying-jib halliards will do to hoist the foremost part of the arch (from the jib-boom end to the foretopmasthead). Care should be taken and taste must be exercised in selecting and placing the flags. Reeve off the three arch halliards and measure the distance in the three clear parts, by marking the halliards, so that you will know what length of flags to bend on, and thus avoid the inconvenience and annoyance of sending the string on deck after they have once been hoisted, for the purpose of alterations. In addition to stopping the flags to the halliards on the head and tack, take a couple of stitches to the halliards about midway. The Jack should be hoisted on the jack-staff on the bowsprit. In reeving off the halliards for the span between the fore and maintop-mastheads, let the ends (or hauling parts) lead through single blocks and down alongside of the fore and main-masts respectively, bending the flags on to the bight, and trice up by the two parts, manned at the same time that the flags are sent aloft. At sunset come up with your outhauls, and the forward and after strings of flags will come inboard, and can then be lowered away. Just before "colors" send the two masthead ensigns aloft "made up". When the signal is made, hoist away on the arch halliards, and, at the instant the flags reach home, "break out" the ensign and the Jack. Pennants and square flags should be bent on alternately. Another mode of dressing ship is by "up and down" flags. That is, by flying a string of flags from each topmast-head to the deck.

# SPECIAL LIGHTS.

Commodore's Lights. Between sunset and colors when on board in harbor the commodore shows two blue lights in globular lanterns suspended perpendicularly at the after gaff-end, or on the flag-pole at the stern. When the commodore is absent one blue light is shown in the same place.

Vice-Commodore's Lights. The vice-commodore shows the the same number of lights as the commodore and in the same place, but the color is red.

Rear-Commodore's Lights. The rear-commodore also shows the same number of lights and in the same place as prescribed for the commodore, but the color is white.

Captain's Light. All captains when on board show one white light in a globular lantern under the main boom. When absent, no light of such character should be shown under the boom. White light in the starboard main spreader indicates that the owner or guests are at dinner.

# OFFICIAL CEREMONIES AND COURTESIES.

**Quarter-deck to be Saluted.** The quarter-deck should always be saluted by officers and men, by raising the cap upon coming over the gangway when boarding their own or another yacht, or a naval vessel.

**Senior Officer to Return Salutes and Visits.** The senior officer present is in command of all the yachts at the anchorage that are flying the burgee of the club he represents, and it is his duty to make and return salutes and visits.

**Senior Officer to Tender Civilities to Visiting Yacht-- Captain of Visiting Yacht to Pay Respects in Person.** When a yacht visits the home waters of another club, and after salutes have been exchanged, the senior officer present representing such home club should send to the visiting yacht a tender of the civilities of the club, after which the captain of the visiting yacht should pay his respects in person to the commanding officer of the anchorage.

**Reception of the President of the United States.** The President of the United States should be received at the gangway of the yacht by the commanding officer of such, and should be piped over the side by the boatswain—the crew being drawn up in line on the port side of the deck. As the President reaches the deck, the President's flag should be broken out at the main-topmast-head and one gun fired from the yacht in salute to same, while the captain, officers and crew should raise their caps in salute. When the President leaves, the crew should be stationed as before and the captain should escort the President to the gangway, where the boatswain should be found as before to blow a pipe and raise his cap, together with the crew, as the President reaches the rail. One gun should be fired and the President's flag hauled down as soon as the boat conveying the President shoves off from the yacht's side. Provided the President embarks in one of the yacht's boats, his flag should be carried on the flag-pole in the bows of the boat while the President is in it, and the yacht's ensign should be carried at the stern, as usual. The sailing master of the yacht should be detailed to take charge of the yacht's boat that carries the President. The captain's gig should always be the boat employed in transporting guests whom it is desired to specially honor.

Reception of the Vice-President of the United States.

The Vice-President of the United States should receive the same honors as prescribed for the President, except that the national flag should be substituted for the President's flag and only one salute fired, which should take place when the Vice-President leaves. A small national flag should be carried on the flag-

27

staff in the bows of the yacht's boat while conveying the Vice-President.

**Reception of the Secretary of the Navy.** The Secretary of the Navy of the United States should receive the same honors as prescribed for the Vice-President, substituting the distinguishing flag of the Secretary.

**Reception of Other Cabinet Officers.** Other Cabinet Officers should receive the same honors as prescribed for the Secretary of the Navy, except that there is no distinguishing or special bunting to be used.

**Reception of the Governor of a State.** The Governor of a State should be received with the same honors as prescribed for the Vice-President, except that the flag of his State should be substituted both at the main-topmast-head and in the bows of the yacht's boats.

**Reception of a Foreign Sovereign.** A foreign sovereign or the chief magistrate of any foreign country should be received on board with the same honors as prescribed for the President of the United States, except that the flag of his country should be substituted.

**Reception of a Member of a Royal family.** A member of a royal family should receive the same honors as prescribed for their sovereign, except that only one salute be fired, which should take place at the time the honored guest leaves the yacht.

**Reception of Naval and Army Officers.** A naval or army officer should be received at the gangway of the yacht by the captain, and should be piped over the side by the boatswain, who should stand alongside the gangway and keep his cap lifted while blowing his pipe. Upon leaving, the captain should escort his guest to the gangway and should observe that the boatswain is stationed as before to wind his call as the officer goes over the yacht's side. If the naval or army officer is of the rank of commander or lieutenant-colonel, or higher, a gun may be fired after the boat containing the guest has shoved off from the yacht's side. Provided the yacht's boat is used by the guest, one of the yacht's officers should be sent in charge of same.

**Reception of Members of the Diplomatic Corps.** Members of the diplomatic corps of the rank of minister should be given the same honors as prescribed for Cabinet Officers, and if below the rank of minister, they should be given the same honors as prescribed for naval and army officers.

**Reception of Other Officials.** Other high officials not mentioned in the foregoing may have such honors accorded them in visiting the yacht as may be consistent with the rules laid down.

**Ceremony of Putting a Yacht in Commission.** The ceremony of putting a yacht in commission is exceedingly simple. As a rule this takes place as soon as the yacht is in proper sailing trim — that is, when the bright-woodwork, etc., is scraped and varnished, standing rigging set up, running rigging rove off, decks cleaned, sails bent, etc. The officers and men appear on deck in uniform, and the club burgee and captain's private signal are "made up" and hoisted to their respective trucks; then the captain (the sailing master may be authorized to act in the former's place) addresses the sailing master: "Mr. ———, I declare the yacht '———' in commission." When this is said, the sailing master orders the burgee and private signal to be "broken out" and the yacht ensign hoisted — this consummates the putting of the yacht in commission.

**Ceremony of Putting the Yacht out of Commission.** The ceremony of going out of commission consists simply of the following: Before the unbending of sail or the dismantling of the yacht in any way, the crew appear on deck in uniform, and the club burgee, private signal and ensign halliards are manned. The owner addresses the sailing master: "Mr. ———, I declare the yacht '———' out of commission." Upon this the sailing master orders a gun to be fired, and the burgee, private signal and ensign lowered. The dismantling of the yacht may then commence.

**Honors to the Captain when Embarking and Disembarking.** When the captain is seen coming off to the yacht, it should so be reported to the sailing master (provided he is on board, and, in his absence, to the mate), who will at once station one of the quarter-masters, or one of the crew, at the "absence flag" halliards, and the boatswain at the gangway to blow a pipe as the captain comes over the side, and, as the gig comes alongside the gangway, the sailing master will face the side, and, as the captain steps over the rail, the sailing master and boatswain will salute by touching the cap visor, and the absence flag will be hauled down. The gig will remain alongside for orders. The sailing master, after ascertaining the captain's wishes in regard to the gig, will either order it hoisted or hauled out to the boom. When intending to leave the ship, the captain should send word to that effect to the sailing master (or to the mate, in the absence of the former), who will see that the gig is dropped down to the starboard gangway and properly manned, when it will then be reported as ready to the captain. The sailing master and boatswain will then take their stations at the gangway, having a hand stationed at the absence flag halliards; and, as the captain passes them to enter the boat, the boatswain will wind his call and touch his cap, and the captain shall receive and return the sailing master's salute. The absence flag will be run up as the boat shoves off.

## SALUTES IN GENERAL.

**Guns Between Sunset and Colors.** Guns fired between sunset and colors are considered signals of distress.

**Guns on Sunday.** Guns should not be fired on Sunday, either in the way of a salute or when getting underway or when coming to anchor.

**Colors and Sunset Gun to be Fired by Senior Officer's Yacht.** When in company with one or more yachts of the same club, the gun fired to make colors or sunset should be that of the yacht of the senior officer of such club present, whether he is on board his vessel or not.

**Yachts to Salute Naval Vessels.** All yachts should salute naval vessels of their own or any other friendly country, by dipping the ensign. It is customary for yachts to salute a naval vessel by dipping the ensign once.

**Dipping the Ensign.** In no case is the ensign to be dipped more than three times in one salute.

**Yachts Passing to Salute.** Yachts passing one another in narrow or inland waters should salute each other by dipping the ensign once — the junior saluting first.

**Yachts Meeting at Sea to Salute.** In meeting at sea, yachts should salute each other, and this salute may consist of simply dipping the ensign three times, or the same may be prefaced by the firing of a gun — but the latter is optional.

**Steam Whistles not to be Used in Saluting.** Steam whistles should not be employed in making or exchanging salutes between steam yachts.

To Salute Upon Entering Harbor.
Upon entering harbor captains should salute the commanding officer of the anchorage by firing one gun or by dipping the ensign at the time the anchor is dropped.

Salute to a Yacht Entering Harbor.
The salute to be made to a yacht entering port and entitled to a salute consists of dipping the ensign once, or the firing of a gun when the arriving yacht drops her anchor.

Special Salute to Commodore Entering Harbor.
On the occasion of the commodore entering harbor to assume personal command of his squadron, he should be saluted on coming to anchor (and not before) by each yacht of the squadron. This salute should consist of the firing of one gun from each yacht or by the dipping of the ensign.

Ordinary Salute to Commodore Entering Harbor.
On ordinary occasions when the commodore's yacht enters harbor his flag should only be saluted with

one gun from the yacht of the senior officer of such club present, or by the dipping of the ensign from such senior's yacht.

**Junior Officer's Yacht Entering Harbor.** When a junior flag officer's yacht enters harbor, his flag should be saluted when his yacht comes to anchor by one gun, or by the dipping of the ensign, from the yacht of the senior officer present, provided the latter is inferior in rank to the arriving flag-officer; otherwise the arriving officer will salute the flag of the officer in command of the anchorage with one gun or by the dipping of the ensign when his yacht drops anchor.

**Senior Officer Leaving Harbor.** A senior officer leaving harbor should indicate that he has transferred his command to the officer next below him in rank, by firing a gun or by dipping his ensign upon getting underway.

**Flag Officer Making Official Visit.** When a flag officer makes an official visit between colors and sunset, his flag should be run up to the fore-topmast-head of the yacht visited and broken out as soon as he boards the same. Upon leaving, one gun should be fired and his flag hauled down after he has entered the boat alongside and it has been shoved off from the yacht.

**Official Salute to Another Club.** An official salute to another club should be made by hoisting the burgee of such club to the fore-topmast-head and firing one gun. After the salute has been returned, or a reasonable time for the return of such allowed, the burgee should be hauled down and the yacht's own burgee hoisted. In the absence of the burgee of the club that is being saluted, the yacht's own burgee may be half-masted while the salute is given.

**Postponed Salutes.** Salutes postponed on account of Sunday, or owing to the arrival of a yacht after sunset, should be made immediately after colors on the following morning.

Judge's Yacht Not to be Saluted. During a race a yacht acting as judge's boat should not be saluted.

Salutes between Squadrons of Different Clubs. When squadrons of different clubs meet, whether in harbor or at sea, salutes should be exchanged only by the commanding officers of such squadrons.

Salutes between Single Yacht and Squadron. Salutes from single yachts to a squadron should be answered only by the commanding officer of the squadron.

Boat Salutes. Salutes to be made between boats will be found under the head of "Boat Service."

# BOAT SERVICE.

## PARTICULARS CONCERNING BOATS.

Boats used on board yachts are known as gigs, cutters, life-boats and dingeys.

Boats are built in three different ways, namely: The *carval-built*, the planks fore and aft, the edges meeting but not overlapping. The *clinker-built*, the planks fore and aft, the edges overlapping. The *diagonal-built*, the planking running diagonally, the inside planks running in a contrary direction to the outside planks, their edges meeting.

Boats are called *single* or *double-banked*, according as they have one or two rowers to a thwart.

*Thwarts* are the seats on which the crew sit; the space abaft the after thwart is called the *stern-sheets*.

The spaces for the oars in the wash streak of boats are called *rowlocks*.

Oars are made of ash or spruce; that part of the oar which is dipped in the water is called the *blade;* the round part which is inboard, the *loom;* the extremity of the loom, which is grasped by the rower's hand, the *handle*.

Oars are called *double-banked* when two men pull one oar.

*Feathering* is known as turning the blades nearly flat to the water after the stroke with the upper edge turned forward.

*Boat-falls* are purchases made with two blocks and a length of rope, used for hoisting a boat to the davits.

The *painter* is a length of line made fast into a ring-bolt in the stem of boats, used for making the boat fast, to tow by, etc.

The *gunwale* of a boat is the upper rail.

The *yoke* is a piece of wood or metal fitted across the head of a boat's rudder.

*Yoke lines* are pieces of rope made fast to the yoke by which the rudder is turned and the boat steered.

*Boat-davits* are pieces of timber or iron projecting over a vessel's sides or stern to hoist boats up to.

A *plug* is the wooden stopper fitted into a hole in the bottom of the boat to let in or keep out water.

*Flooring* is the bottom boards of the boat.

*Boat-booms* are the booms on either side of a vessel to which the boats ride when the ship is at anchor.

A *Boat-breaker* is a small keg used for carrying fresh water.

A *Boat-recall* is an understood signal made from the ship to summon a boat to return.

*Gripes* are long strips of canvas leading from the davit ends, and passing under a boat to secure it. They are set taut by lanyards.

*Boat-fenders* are small shapes of canvas or leather stuffed and hung over a boat's side to prevent it from being chafed and from chafing the sides of the yacht.

*Back Board* is a board in the stern of the boat on which is often printed the name of the yacht to which she belongs.

## BOAT CEREMONY AND DISCIPLINE.

The lading of the gig should be arranged so that juniors in rank and in official importance should enter the boat first, and the one highest in rank and importance should immediately precede the captain, who should always be the last to enter the boat and the first to disembark. The disembarking should take place in the reverse order to the embarking, so that the junior in rank should be the last to leave the boat.

## BOAT ORDERS.

In the following the gig is supposed to be manned, and lying alongside the gangway.

After the gig is reported ready to the captain, he will direct his guests to enter the boat, and after they are all seated he will receive and return the sailing-master's salute, then take his place in the gig — care having been observed to leave the sternsheets clear for him, and the yoke lines ready to hand.

The captain will observe that his private signal is stepped in the bows, that the seating of his guests does not interfere with the stroke oarsman, and will then call:
"Shove off Forward!"
When this order is given, the man in the bows shoves the boat's head away from

the ship's side, stows his boat-hook, and lays his hands on his oar.

The next order is: "Up Oars!" "Oars Apeak" is sometimes wrongfully employed.

The crew will simultaneously seize and raise their proper oars briskly to the vertical (keeping their eyes on the stroke oarsman), and hold them thus directly in front of them, the blades being fore-and-aft, the ends of the oars held clear of the boat's bottom; the oarsmen sitting on the port side of the boat holding the oars with right hands down, and those sitting on the starboard side holding the oars with left hands down. The oarsmen sitting on the port side of the boat pull the starboard oars, and the oarsmen sitting on the starboard side of the boat pull the port oars.

The next command is: "Let Fall!"

The oars must be dropped into the rowlocks together, care being taken to prevent the blades from striking the water — blades flat to the water and leveled.

Next give the order: "Give Way!"

The boat is now underway, the crew taking the style of pulling from the stroke oarsman.

In running alongside of a vessel or float-stage, give the boat sufficient impetus to "reach"; then call, while the blades are in the water: "Way Enough!"

The men will finish the stroke and then raise their oars simultaneously to a vertical position, and lay them with as little noise as possible amidships in the boat in a line with the keel, the blades pointing forward. The stroke and bow oarsmen seize their boat-hooks, and as the boat runs alongside they stop its way and hold it.

With four or more oared boat, just before the order "Way Enough" is given, the order "In Bow" should be given to allow the man forward to get in his oar and take his boat-hook in hand ready to fend off when the boat comes alongside the landing.

## BOAT SALUTES.

Flag officers should display their pennants in the bows of boats when underway, captains their private signals, and members the club burgee.

Only boats displaying pennants, private signals or burgees are entitled to a salute from another boat.

Junior flag officers, captains, and members in command of boats, should order their crews to temporarily lie on their oars to the commodore's boat in passing, and at the same time should raise their cap in salute. Captains and members in command of boats should also salute junior flag officers in the same manner as prescribed for the commodore.

Sailing-masters, under-officers and coxswains should order their crews to lie on their oars to all boats passing that display a pennant, private signal or club burgee, and shall raise the cap in salute.

Seniors in rank acknowledge salutes by simply raising the cap, and do not cease rowing.

Captains passing should salute each other by raising the cap—the junior saluting first—but the crews will not lie on their oars.

The salutes from all boats under sail, being towed, or laden, should be made by the one in charge raising his cap, and the way of such boats should not be checked.

When approaching your own or another yacht for the purpose of going alongside, on being hailed, answer by giving the name of your yacht if a captain, but if a commodore, the reply should be "Flag."

If it is desired to cease rowing temporarily, give the order: "Oars!" The crew will then lift the blades of their oars from the water, holding the blades horizontally, and at right angles to the keel.

When it is desired to continue rowing, simply call: "Give Way!"

When rowing, if passing so close to another boat that a collision of oars seems probable, call: "Trail!" The men will keep their oars in the rowlocks, but permit the blades to trail aft and alongside. When the danger is past, call: "Oars!" — this brings the crew to attention with the oars in position to receive the order: "Give Way!"

Never allow a boat's crew to splash the water with the blades of their oars when the order to "let fall" is executed.

Talking among a boat's crew, or turning the head to observe any object while the boat is underway, should never be allowed.

The starboard after oar is called the "stroke oar", and gives the stroke, the remainder of the crew taking the style from it; consequently, it should be manned by the best man in the boat — the coxswain of a gig pulls the stroke oar when the captain is in the boat.

In rowing, the blade of each oar should be lifted as high as the gunwale after it leaves the water, then feathered by dropping the wrist. A short pause should then be made, and the oar next thrown well forward, and dropped edgewise into the water, taking care to avoid splashing. Now, rip the oar through the water with a hearty swing, and then repeat as above.

If it is required to turn a boat suddenly, or short round to starboard, then give the order to "Give Way Port; Back Starboard". If it is required to turn short to port, then,

"Give Way Starboard; Back Port". When the boat is pointed aright, then, "Give Way Together".

In backing, as in pulling, the crew should always keep stroke with the after oar of their respective sides.

Never send a boat away from a ship at night without being provided with a lantern, as many a boat has been run down through inability to make its presence known.

Remember, in running alongside a ship or landing, that the deeper the boat is freighted, the longer she will carry her way in the water.

In leaving a ship in foggy weather, provide the boat with a fog-horn and compass, and judge as nearly as possible the bearing of the landing you wish to make. Take the opposite of this bearing to return to the ship, making in both cases due allowance for tide.

The boats should always be kept in perfect condition, and, unless the crew are required to shift themselves, not more than three minutes should elapse between the time the boat is called away and its arrival at the gangway, manned and ready.

Never send away a gig's crew unless they are dressed alike, and look "spick and span". Hat ribbons should always be worn by a boat's crew.

Nothing shows the good discipline of a yacht more than efficient boat service; and it is worthy of all pains and consideration.

The ranking officer should always be the last to enter a boat, and the first to leave it. He will, also, command the boat.

To ride out a gale of wind in an open boat, lash the oars and bottom boards together and weight them if possible. Span them with the boat's painter and pitch them overboard. This will keep the boat head to the sea and prevent it from drifting fast.

Assist the boat to keep head to the sea by the use of a steering oar.

When crossing the bar of a river, if the water is much troubled, a steering oar should be used, and the rudder unshipped.

In the case of a boat being unable to pull up to the ship against a strong wind or tide, veer a line out from the ship with the end made fast to a buoy or any floating material sufficient to sustain the bight, and when this reaches the boat the crew can make the end of the line fast to the ring in the stem, and the boat can then be hauled up. Another way is to drop a boat astern with a line secured to its painter and then haul them both up together.

When two boats are approaching the same gangway, or landing stage, the junior officer in rank should always give way to the senior.

# SHIP'S BELLS.

The manner of telling the time on board ship is by striking the bell. Eight bells indicate midnight, 4 A. M., 8 A. M., noon, 4 P. M., and 8 P. M. Thus it will be seen that every even four hours after midnight brings 8 bells around. After midnight the first bell struck is 1, which stands for half-past twelve; one o'clock is represented by 2 bells, half-past one, by 3 bells; two o'clock by 4 bells; half-past two, by 5 bells; three o'clock, by 6 bells; half-past three, by 7 bells; and four o'clock, by 8 bells.

At half-past four 1 bell is struck, and so on, in the above order, until eight o'clock is made known by 8 bells again.

*TABLE.*

*Midnight . . . . . . 8 bells.*
*12.30 A. M. . . . . . 1 bell.*

| | | |
|---|---|---|
| 1.00 | A. M. | 2 bells. |
| 1.30 | "     | 3   "    |
| 2.00 | "     | 4   "    |
| 2.30 | "     | 5   "    |
| 3.00 | "     | 6   "    |
| 3.30 | "     | 7   "    |
| 4.00 | "     | 8   "    |

# THE BOATSWAIN'S CALL.

On vessels where a good-sized crew is carried, the "Boatswain's Call" should be largely employed.

The following should always be "piped":

The call to meals; the order to heave round; to order away boats; the order to haul; the order to belay; the order to man the side; the order to make colors; the order to make sunset; to call all hands; the call to muster; to pipe down.

It is impossible to explain on paper the regular man-o'-wars-man's "pipe" for the different orders, nor is it necessary that their style should be followed out strictly on yachts — any understood combination between the boatswain (or mate) and the crew will answer all the purposes for which the "call" is intended.

The following is offered:

*The Call of Attention:* A long straight pipe. This is used as a preface to the verbal call of all hands on deck or to muster.

*To Call Away a Boat:* A long straight pipe, followed by the verbal order: "Away gig!" (or dingey, or cutter, as the case may be).

*The Call to Meals:* Three long, rolling pipes.

*To Heave Round, or to Pull:* Several moderately short, straight pipes.

*To Belay:* Two short, quick chirps, followed by a moderately short rolling pipe.

*To Pipe the Side:* A prolonged straight pipe. (The boatswain stands facing the gangway, his "call" held to his mouth with his left hand, while his right hand is raised to his cap in salute.) This pipe should be made to the captain, when coming on board or when leaving the yacht. It should also be made to all other yacht commanders, dignitaries, and officers of the army and navy.

*To Make "Colors" or "Sunset":* Two short, quick chirps, followed by a long, rolling pipe.

*To Pipe Down:* One long, straight, followed by a long, rolling pipe.

# YACHT ROUTINE.

As soon as a yacht is put in commission, the organization of the officers and crew should be considered, so that everything may work smoothly and harmoniously, to the satisfaction and peace of the captain and the manifest benefit of all concerned. The sailing-master should be held responsible for this, and, in perfecting the details, of course, he must be guided by the number of his crew.

If, in washing down, cleaning bright work, etc., each man is given a certain station and allotted a particular piece of work, it will be found that matters will be greatly expedited, and the individual tasks will be performed better, for the reason that the man is held accountable for the appearance of his own part of the ship.

Silence is one of the best evidences of discipline, and the officers should set the example to the crew. When it is necessary to issue an order let it be done in a quiet tone and avoid calling along the deck as much as possible. The latter suggests the "coaster" and establishes a bad precedent.

When in port, the last anchor watch should turn out the cook one hour before "all hands", so that morning coffee may be ready when the general call is made.

Allow but twenty minutes between "turn out" and "turn to".

After pumping the bilges, wash down decks, wipe the sides around and the bright wood of the rail skylights and companion way and then turn all hands on to the brass work, using a chamois skin.

Three-quarters of an hour should be given the crew for breakfast, after which they should again be turned to, the brass work finished, the decks tidied up, the crew dressed in their ordered uniform for the day and everything ready for inspection by the sailing-master and captain (if the latter so desires.)

The sailing-master (or mate) should always have one of the men row him around the vessel the last thing in the morning, to make sure that all the running rigging is taut, no scratches or chafing on the sides; that there are no evidences of grass or scum along the water line, and that everything is proper and ship-shape.

One hour should be allowed for men for dinner — from 12 to 1.

A good sailing-master will always find something for the crew to work at during working hours.

Smoking should never be allowed between decks.

Smoking hours on deck should be regulated.

Never allow smoking while the crew are at work about the decks.

After supper (in port) allow the crew to smoke on the forward deck as long as they please.

Under no consideration ever permit a boat's crew to smoke while in the boat.

In sending any boat ashore, the sailing-master (or, in his absence, the mate) should always direct the boat where to land, and when to return to the ship, except when the captain is in the gig, who will direct his own crew.

The crew should be habituated to move smartly about the decks, and to answer quickly and respectfully to their officers.

In passing the captain the crew should always salute by touching the right hand to the cap.

Mattresses and blankets should be thoroughly aired once every week, and oftener should there have been damp weather.

The sailing-master and mates should never be ashore at the same time while the yacht is in commission.

When coming to anchor, have the men stationed, and the instant the anchor leaves the cat head, fire a gun and swing out the boat booms.

When leaving anchorage, if a steam yacht, fire a gun the instant the anchor is aweigh, and the bell is rung to go ahead, but if a sailing yacht, fire a gun when the anchor is tripped, and the vessel fills away.

On large yachts a quarter-master should always be on watch to give notice to the officer of the deck on the approach of boats to the vessel, signals made from other yachts, or from the shore.

*Underway at Night:* Always have a lookout stationed forward, and in case of unusual darkness or thick weather, it is better to have two lookouts—one on either bow. As soon as a light or a sail is sighted it should be reported in clear, sharp tones to the officer of the deck, who will at once convince himself as to its character and whether his vessel or the one reported has the "right of way", and act accordingly.

*At Anchor at Night:* As soon as it is dark the "anchor watch" should be set. According to the number of the crew available, the length of time for each man to guard the deck should be regulated, so that from the time the first anchor watch is set until all hands are called in the morning, the watches shall be uniform, and no one man called on deck twice during the night. It is the duty of the watch to keep continually on the alert, examining the moorings occasionally, visiting the quarter-deck, keeping an eye to the bright burning of the anchor light, observing the drift lead, the swinging of his own vessel with the tide, also of the vessels around him, and being careful that no boat gets alongside his vessel unawares. In case a boat is seen making for the yacht, it should be hailed — "Boat-Ahoy!" and, if the hail is answered satisfactorily, the boat can be allowed to board; but, if not, it must be warned off. In case of danger, pound on the top of the forecastle slide with anything available, at the same time calling "All Hands!" in a voice calculated to rouse the sleepers, and then, until the deck is officered, act yourself under the circumstances, as your common sense dictates. The anchor watch should strike the bells regularly during the night.

*Concerning Watches:* As soon as a yacht leaves port, bound on a voyage, the crew should be divided into watches and the first regular watch set at 8 P. M. on the day of sailing. The captain always takes the first watch out, and the sailing-master the first watch home. The stewards, cooks, and waiters are known as "idlers" and they stand no watch.

The captain's watch is called the "starboard" and the sailing-master's the "port" watch.

If there is an uneven number of men in the forecastle, the odd man goes into the captain's watch by courtesy.

Provided the yacht carries a mate, the captain's watch is kept by him, so that the captain has no regular deck duty, but goes and comes as he pleases.

The officer on watch is known as the "officer of the deck", and, while left in possession, his orders must be obeyed to the letter. He has full powers to alter the course of the ship to avoid danger, to make or alter, or take in sail, etc.

The seven regular watches are named as follows :

From midnight to 4 A. M., . *the Mid Watch*
" 4 A. M. to 8 A. M., *the Morning Watch*
" 8 A. M. to noon, *the Forenoon Watch*
" noon to 4 P. M., *the Afternoon Watch*
" 4 P. M. to 6 P. M., *the First Dog Watch*
" 6 P. M. to 8 P. M., *the Second Dog Watch*
" 8 P. M. to 12 midnight, *the First Watch*

# DUTIES AND RESPONSIBILITIES OF OFFICERS.

*Note.*

In the following treatise on the duties and responsibilities of the Captain and his officers, the question of the steam yacht carrying a goodly crew has been particularly considered; but the rules, regulations, etc., laid down for the government of such large craft may easily be modified and brought within the compass of smaller steam and sail yachts.

## THE CAPTAIN.

The sailing-master, mates, boatswain, carpenter, engineers, stewards, the petty officers, such as quartermasters, cooks, oilers, boatswain's mates, etc., as well as every seaman, fireman, and waiter on board the yacht are subject to the control and orders of the Captain.

The Captain is responsible for the general equipment and general management of his yacht, and for the vessel (when in commission) being at all times fully found and provided with coals, water, provisions, compasses, chronometers, charts, sextants, and other stores and appliances requisite for the navigation of the yacht. Of course, these duties may be assigned to the sailing-master by the Captain, but upon the latter rests the responsibility of giving the necessary orders to insure such performance.

The Captain shall inspect the yacht every day to observe that cleanliness and order is practised in the various departments—deck, engineer and stewards—and shall hold strictly accountable for each department the officer in charge of same.

The Captain shall see to it that the officers attend strictly to their several duties, that no waste or extravagance in the way of stores and provisions is allowed, and that the men under the different heads of the departments are respectful and obedient to their superiors and move smartly in the discharge of their duties.

The Captain will observe that the officers and men respect the laws and regulations of the ports visited by the yacht, and will issue strict orders that contraband or dutiable articles for personal use shall not be brought on board to cause trouble and annoyance upon the return of the yacht to a home port, or upon an attempt to smuggle such articles ashore in any other port.

The Captain shall see to it that the crew are frequently exercised at fire-quarters, and shall enforce the order that all boats are kept ready for immediate lowering and that the fire-hose is attached at night and ready for use at a moment's notice.

The Captain will exact the observance of strict courtesy between the officers of various departments and not allow undue familiarity between them outside of their own quarters, and gambling between the officers or between the men shall always be prohibited.

The Captain will forbid private trading on the part of officers and crew under any circumstances, and shall impress upon the minds of all on board that the dignity of a gentleman's private vessel is to be upheld, and that loud or vulgar language will not be tolerated.

The Captain will have reported to him all cases of misconduct on the part of any of the crew, and will never permit punishment to be inflicted unless by his express orders, and he will award the character of the punishment after consulting with the sailing-master, engineer or steward, according to the department in which the offender belongs. He is responsible for any ill-treatment of the crew by his officers.

If one of the crew die on board, the Captain must make an inventory of his effects, entering same with the name, rank, etc., in the log-book, and upon the arrival of the yacht in port, a report must be made to the health-officer of the port.

The Captain has the power to appoint his officers and has entire command over them during the time they are on board. He may, for any cause, suspend them from duty, and in the case of mutinous conduct at sea he is justified in putting in irons any officer, or any member of the crew. The log-book must, according to law, set forth all that occurs of an important nature during the voyage, especially such cases as punishment inflicted, and for what cause, etc.

Upon arrival in a foreign port, the Captain should go to the Custom House, taking the bill-of-health and yacht's papers and report his arrival.

## THE SAILING - MASTER.

Under the head of "Yacht Routine", in a preceding chapter, will be found in detail the character of the deck work that the sailing-master should see carried out.

The sailing-master, when the yacht is underway, will never allow the officer of the deck to leave the bridge unless regularly or temporarily relieved.

If the sailing-master disapproves of anything performed by one of the officers, he should quietly call him aside and correct him, but he should never do it within the hearing of the crew, as they may lose respect for an officer who was not shown respect by an officer above him.

The sailing-master, mate, second mate, or any other officer, when in charge of the deck has full power over the yacht, as he represents the authority of the Captain.

The sailing-master will navigate the yacht and will be responsible to the Captain for the safety and order of the vessel above and below decks, and, provided he is entrusted to select the officers and crew, he will be responsible to the Captain for their competency and desirability in all respects.

Whenever an officer, or any of the seamen, desires to see the Captain for personal reasons, he must first acquaint the sailing-master with his wishes, and the sailing-master will refer the request to the Captain, who will specify his pleasure in the matter, and such will be conveyed in turn to the applicant; but under no circumstances will the Captain be approached by an officer or man, "over the sailing-master's head", for the only way to maintain discipline on board is by impressing upon the crew as a whole that the sailing-master, being the executive officer, the running of the yacht is in his hands, and the most implicit obedience and respect must be accorded him.

Officers and men must never think of leaving the yacht, even when alongside the dock, without first obtaining the consent of the sailing-master, or, in his absence, from the officer left in command, who will be acquainted with the sailing-master's wishes in the matter.

When entering or leaving port, the sailing-master's place is on the bridge, directing the movements of the yacht.

## CHIEF ENGINEER.

The chief engineer has full control over all persons — officers and men — in his department.

The engineer on watch in the engine-room when the yacht is underway, represents the chief engineer, and the fireman on watch must obey him, and he in turn must obey any orders received from the officer of the deck in the way of handling the engines.

The chief engineer will be held responsible for all hands in his department implicitly carrying out the orders of the Captain, or of the officer of the deck.

Neither the assistants nor any member of the engine or fire-room force will leave the vessel without first reporting to and obtaining the chief engineer's consent, who, in turn, will solicit the same from the sailing-master and then acquaint the applicant with the result.

The chief engineer will personally superintend the coaling of the yacht, and satisfy himself that the quantity of coal charged for has been received on board. He will make an entry on the engine-room log-book stating the amount of coal receipted for, also its quality.

When other engine-room stores, tools, etc., are received on board, they will be receipted for by the chief engineer and a memorandum of same entered on his log-book.

The chief engineer will be held responsible for any waste of stores or extravagance in his department.

The chief engineer will be held accountable for the conduct of all officers and men under his control.

The chief engineer will enforce the law that an engineer on watch is never to absent himself from the engine-room without having been regularly relieved by another engineer, and will also see to it that no fireman, oiler, water-tender, etc., leaves his post without permission from the engineer on watch.

Should any member of the engineer's force misconduct himself, or disobey any order received by him from a superior officer, the chief engineer must report the case to the Captain, so that it may be dealt with by the latter, and in no case is the chief or one of his assistants to inflict punishment upon a man unless such punishment is authorized by the Captain.

The chief engineer will see to it that the engineer of the watch keeps a steady pressure of steam according to the instructions that he has received, and with a view to economy of fuel, the engineer on watch will direct attention to the condition of the fires, and the mode of firing. The chief will also make sure that his assistants are well acquainted with the various pipes, cocks, valves and connections generally.

When entering or leaving port the chief engineer will assume personal charge of the engines or at any other time when special care is demanded for executing promptly the orders signalled from the bridge.

The chief engineer will keep the engine-room log-book and fill up the columns therein. Under the head of "Remarks" he will enter the particulars of all stores used; the time of leaving and arriving in port; all occurrences relating to the working of the boilers and machinery, accidents of whatever nature to engines or to the men, etc., and each day's log is to be verified by his signature.

The chief engineer will daily, at noon, while under steam, lay before the sailing-master an abstract of the engine-room logbook, containing the expenditure of coals, oils and other stores during the preceding twenty-four hours, and the amount remaining on hand; also the total number of revolutions made during the preceding twenty-four hours.

The chief engineer will be held responsible that the steam steering-gear, windlass, refrigerating and electric plants are kept in efficient state and at all times ready when required.

On sailing days, or on departure from any port, the chief engineer must have his department in good order, steam maintained at the proper limit, and half an hour before the time of starting, he must report to the sailing-master that his department is all ready, after which the chief and his assistants must remain on duty until the yacht is clear of the pilot or the harbor cleared, when the first assistant engineer will take charge of the engine-room watch.

Should the engineer of the watch find it necessary to stop his engines when underway, he shall at once send word to the sailing-master or to the officer of the deck, and obtain his consent before stopping, except in cases of special emergency, when he will be justified in stopping without orders, but knowledge of the act must at once be sent to the officer of the deck.

The chief engineer will have full control of regulating the amount of steam to be carried, using his own judgment as to what is necessary for the speed required.

## FIRST MATE.

It is common to refer to the first mate as the "chief-officer".

After being appointed the chief-officer, he should get an inventory of everything under his charge, and obtain from the boatswain and carpenter a list of their stores also, and a memorandum of whatever else they require. He should see that the windlass is in good working order, and inspect personally the boats, falls, running and standing rigging, sails, sail-covers, awnings, etc., and each night should lay out the work for the boatswain and give him orders concerning his work for the coming day. He should also observe that the carpenter attends to the sluices and sounds the well and tanks night and morning.

When underway at sea, if the chief-officer does not stand watch, he should be about the decks all day to see that the boatswain is pushing the work along.

The chief-officer will also keep the log-book, copying into it from the rough or deck log, and should take sights of the sun for latitude and longitude, determine the deviation by azimuths of the sun, and keep the yacht's run by dead-reckoning. The log-book must be ready each day at 2 bells, (one o'clock P. M.), for inspection by the sailing-master.

In anchoring, mooring and unmooring ship, the chief-officer's place is on the forecastle, directing the handling of the bow-lines.

When heaving up anchor, or when coming to anchor, the chief-officer's place is on the forecastle directing the handling of the cable according to orders from the sailing-master on the bridge.

If the first officer stands deck watch, his bridge duties will be the same as those laid down for the second officer.

---

## SECOND MATE.

In mooring and unmooring ship, the second officer's place is aft, and he is responsible for any accident that occurs at his end of the yacht while docking or leaving dock, or when getting underway or coming to anchor.

When running out lines, or taking them in, he must be careful to keep them clear of the propeller, and in the event of a line getting foul of same he must at once make same known to the officer on the bridge so that the engines may be stopped.

When docking, a couple of cork-fenders should be kept handy on the quarters.

After mooring, the ropes should be coiled down neatly, and chafing gear put on where necessary, after which the men should be sent forward to the boatswain.

When leaving port, the second mate should attend to the secure lashing of anything requiring it aft, and also see to it that the carpenter has secured the gangways, ports, etc.

When coming to anchor, the second mate's place is by the leadsman, when he does not take the lead himself.

When at sea, before he relieves the bridge, he should take a turn around the deck fore and aft to see that there is nothing adrift and no evidences· of anything wrong.

He should never hesitate to call the Captain if in doubt about anything of an important nature — such as fog; if weather looks threatening; if the barometer is unsteady; if there is the sight or sound of broken water.

The second mate must be particular to note everything correctly in the log-book for his watch, reading the patent log the last thing and entering the distance run for the preceding four hours.

## BOATSWAIN.

Upon reporting for duty the boatswain must ascertain the kind and quantity of the deck stores, cordage, sails, canvas, paints, brushes, salt-water-soap, brooms, etc., etc., because it is his duty to serve out such in keeping the yacht in order.

He must inspect every time they are used cat-falls, mooring-lines, etc., and if they are found defective, he must at once make a report to the first mate.

The boatswain remains on deck all day and takes charge of all the men engaged on deck work, receiving his orders each night from the first mate as to the character of the work to be carried on the following day; but he must also exercise his own judgment when he sees anything of a minor nature in his department requiring attention.

## CARPENTER.

Upon reporting for duty the carpenter must overhaul all the sluices to see that they are in proper working order; make himself familiar with the location of the sounding-pipe, water tanks, etc.

He must also thoroughly understand the working of the windlass, and take personal charge of it when the anchors are being used. It is his special duty also to examine all dead-lights for leaks, and to attend to the shipping and unshipping of the gangway ladders.

The carpenter is under the direct orders of the chief-officer, and whenever the carpenter's services are required by the engineers, the chief-officer must have the application for the carpenter's services made to him.

The carpenter must sound the tanks and well every night and morning, note his remarks on the engine-room slate, and report as well to the officer of the deck—this must be done both at sea and in port.

It is also the carpenter's duty to attend to the steering-gear and report at once to the chief mate any defect in the wheel-chains or mechanism.

The carpenter has the keeping in repair of all the boats, spars, bulwarks, blocks, and in fact everything of a wooden nature on board the yacht.

## QUARTERMASTERS.

The duties of quartermasters are to steer the yacht, keep the pilot house in order, clean all bright work belonging to his department in the way of binnacles, wheel, speaking tubes, steering-gear, step-plates, etc. They have charge of the bunting and are responsible for its condition, and it is also required of them that they shall be familiar with the signal code, and shall take the signal halliards under their personal care to insure their readiness for use. All the signal lanterns are under their charge, as is also the hand and deep-sea leads. When the yacht is at anchor, quartermasters stand regular watch and watch by day as well as by night, taking charge of the anchor watch.

## STEWARD.

The duties of the steward are varied, and the comfort and happiness of the yacht depend upon his ability, integrity, and ambition to keep a contented ship fore and aft.

Whether he is serving on a small yacht or a large one, he should remember that the money of the millionaire owner should not be any more recklessly spent by the steward than the money of the man who can afford yachting in only a very modest way. Besides this, the steward should be a man of sufficiently high moral character to realize that waste of any kind is wicked.

It matters not how rich an owner may be, he is just as sensitive to the foolish expenditure of his money as is his less pretentious yachting friend, and no steward should conduct his department on the theory that the owner is too well off to be at all concerned whether it costs five dollars a day to provision the yacht or five hundred.

There are stewards who personally are strictly honest, but who are either careless in the quantity of the purchases, or who leave entirely too much to the cook — who think it too great a trouble to look into "pots and pans", or who avoid any such supervision for fear of offending the autocrat of the galley. This is all wrong. The cook is under the direction and orders of the steward, and if the latter is the proper sort of official he will not allow any other interpretation of his authority.

If under-stewards are carried, they are simply aids to the steward, whose orders they will at all times unquestionably obey, and to insure the smooth running of this department, the owner should authorize the steward to select his subordinates.

It goes without saying that all the provisions on board are under his care, and that he should at all times know the amount of stores on hand in his department. He should keep an expenditure book showing credit and debit sides, so as to be able quickly to know how much money he has received from the owner, and what amount of same he has expended.

In addition to his care of the owner's wardrobe, the silverware, glass, crockery, bedding and linen both in the cabins and officers' quarters, he is responsible also for fixtures in the way of lamps, cushions, furniture, etc.

He should, in addition to his supervision of the cabins, inspect the officers' rooms every morning to see that same are sweet and clean. He must demand that everything in the kitchen is kept shining; that the brass-work on the inside of all skylights to cabin and officers' quarters, and the handrails to companionway are at all times carefully polished.

Whenever it is desired to brush rugs and mats on deck, he should always notify the mate so that proper precautions may be taken to prevent dust from injuring anything about decks in the way of fresh paint, varnish, etc.

When it is necessary that he should go ashore for provisions, ice, etc., he should notify the sailing-master sufficiently ahead of time so that the boat-service required may not interfere with the regular deck work.

In the case of guests his duty is to contribute in every way possible to their comfort and pleasure while on board, realizing that by so doing he is not only fulfilling another of his functions, but that he is rendering the greatest satisfaction to the owner, whose pleasure it is to know that the outing offered his friends is being made as pleasant as possible.

## SURGEON.

In the event of a surgeon being carried, it will be the duty of this officer to look after the general health of all on board, and to be keenly alive to the sanitary condition of the yacht.

Whenever an inspection of the vessel is being held, it is his place to accompany the Captain on his rounds, and to offer needful suggestions.

When the yacht's water-tanks are to be filled, he should inspect the quality of the water offered, and should analyze same if he is suspicious that it may be unhealthy owing to the presence of vegetable matter, etc.

Should sickness occur among the crew, he should take proper precautions to isolate the man so far as possible until a satisfactory diagnosis of the case assures him as to the character of the illness.